Patterns at School

Bela Davis

Abdo Kids Junior
is an Imprint of Abdo Kids
abdopublishing.com

Abdo
PATTERNS ARE FUN!
Kids

abdopublishing.com

Published by Abdo Kids, a division of ABDO, P.O. Box 398166, Minneapolis, Minnesota 55439.
Copyright © 2019 by Abdo Consulting Group, Inc. International copyrights reserved in all countries.
No part of this book may be reproduced in any form without written permission from the publisher.
Abdo Kids Junior™ is a trademark and logo of Abdo Kids.

Printed in the United States of America, North Mankato, Minnesota.

052018

092018

 THIS BOOK CONTAINS
RECYCLED MATERIALS

Photo Credits: iStock, Shutterstock

Production Contributors: Teddy Borth, Jennie Forsberg, Grace Hansen

Design Contributors: Christina Doffing, Candice Keimig, Dorothy Toth

Library of Congress Control Number: 2017917624

Publisher's Cataloging-in-Publication Data

Names: Davis, Bela, author.

Title: Patterns at school / by Bela Davis.

Description: Minneapolis, Minnesota : Abdo Kids, 2019. | Series: Patterns are fun! |
    Includes glossary, index and online resources (page 24).

Identifiers: ISBN 9781532107931 (lib.bdg.) | ISBN 9781532108914 (ebook) |
    ISBN 9781532109409 (Read-to-me ebook)

Subjects: LCSH: Pattern perception--Juvenile literature. | School environment--Juvenile literature. |
    Mathematics--Miscellanea--Juvenile literature.

Classification: DDC 006.4--dc23

Table of Contents

Patterns at School

Patterns are all around.

They are even at school!

A pattern is something that is repeated. A lot of things can make a pattern.

Tim makes a pattern with school supplies.

A backpack can have a pattern. Amy's has stripes. Mia's has polka dots.

Kayla plays music. She makes a **series** of sounds. Ba, bing, da, da. Ba, bing, da, da.

Dan **practices** writing.

The lines make a pattern.

Ella plays hopscotch at recess.

The numbers make a pattern.

The squares do too.

Here comes the bus!
Buses show a **series**
of colors and shapes.

18

Look around you. What patterns do you see?

21

Some Types of Patterns

color pattern

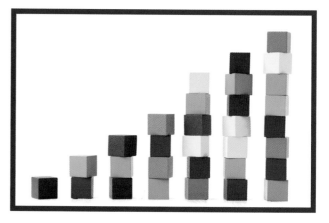

growth pattern

letter pattern

position pattern

Glossary

practice
to do many times in order to become good at it.

series
a group of related things that come one after another.

Index

Abdo Kids
ONLINE
FREE! ONLINE MULTIMEDIA RESOURCES

Visit **abdokids.com** and use this code to access crafts, games, videos, and more!

Abdo Kids Code:
PPK7931

24